S₁

Wild

: From Lost to Found on the Pacific Crest Trail

by Cheryl Strayed

: This is a quick read summary based on the book "Wild : From Lost to Found on the Pacific Crest Trail" by Cheryl Strayed

Note to Readers:

This is a Summary & Analysis of "Wild : From Lost to Found on the Pacific Crest Trail" by Cheryl Strayed. You are encouraged to buy the full version.

Copyright 2015 **by** ABookADay. All rights reserved worldwide. No part of this publication may be reproduced or transmitted in any form without the prior written consent of the publisher.

TABLE OF CONTENTS

OVERVIEW

SUMMARY

PART ONE: The Ten Thousand Things

Chapter 1: The Ten Thousand Things

Chapter 2: Splitting

Chapter 3: Hunching in a Remotely Upright Position

PART TWO: Tracks

Chapter 4: The Pacific Crest Trail, Volume 1: California

Chapter 5: Tracks

Chapter 6: A Bull in Both Directions

Chapter 7: The Only Girl in the Woods

PART THREE: Range of Light

Chapter 8: Corvidology

Chapter9: Staying Found

Chapter 10: Range of Light

PART FOUR: Wild

Chapter 11: The Lou Out of Lou

Chapter 12: This Far

Chapter 13: The Accumulation of Trees

Chapter 14: Wild

PART FIVE: Box of Rain

Chapter 15: Box of Rain

Chapter 16: Mazama

Chapter 17: Into a Primal Gear

Chapter 18: Queen of the PCT

Chapter 19: The Dream of a Common Language

ANALYSIS

OVERVIEW

Wild: From Lost to Found on the Pacific Crest Trail by Cheryl Strayed is a memoir that details the journey of a single woman on the Pacific Crest Trail on a search for meaning after devastating personal losses. In 1995, four years after the death of her mother, and recently divorced, Cheryl Strayed backpacked into the wilderness unprepared for the journey that awaited. This review includes a detailed summary of her tale, followed by a brief analysis.

Cheryl Strayed has written essays for the *New York Times*, *The Washington Post Magazine*, *Salon*, *Vogue* and *The Sun*. She is also the author of the *Dear Sugar* advice column and co-host of the WBUR podcast by the same name. She has a bachelor's from the University of Minnesota and an MFA in fiction from Syracuse University. *Wild* is a New York Times bestselling memoir and was selected for Oprah's Book Club. It has also been adapted as a movie starring Reese Witherspoon.

SUMMARY

PART ONE: THE TEN THOUSAND THINGS

CHAPTER 1: THE TEN THOUSAND THINGS

The author locates the beginning of her journey on the Pacific Crest Trail (PCT) with the death of her mother four and a half years before she stepped foot on the trail itself. Her mother was diagnosed with late stage lung cancer, to the disbelief of her family, as a 45 year old otherwise healthy nonsmoker. The author was 22 at the time and she was very close to her mother. Doctors predicted that she had less than a year to live and that nothing could be done other than to make her as comfortable as possible while the disease progressed.

Strayed was the middle child with an older sister, Karen, and younger brother, Leif. Their biological father, whom their mother married at 19, was physically abusive. She managed to leave him at 28 and worked several jobs until meeting Eddie who would become the children's stepfather. Eddie did construction work and not long after they were married he suffered a fall from a roof and broke his back. They used the settlement money to buy 40 acres of land in a remote area outside of Duluth. There was no house, running water or electricity on the property. Within six months they had built a small one room shack from scrap wood. Eddie took a construction job that kept him living in town, but the children and their mother lived alone on the land. They had a huge garden and raised food to sustain them throughout the year. They used camp stoves and iceboxes and talked to each other in the dark until they fell asleep. There was a deep connection forged to the land and nature in her childhood that the author would try to reconnect with in her journey on the PCT.

When Strayed left for college at St. Thomas in the Twin Cities, her mother took advantage of the free tuition offered to parents of students to pursue her own degree. Both of the women shared a major in women's studies while Strayed also majored in English, her mother in history. They were both seniors when her mother was diagnosed. The progression of the disease was rapid, and Strayed became her mother's primary care giver. Her siblings were not able to share in the responsibilities because it was too difficult to see their mother in this condition. In fact, Leif, who was just 18, was dodging the family's attempt to get in touch with him. One day after her mother was in hospice care and seemed to be approaching the end, Strayed made a final effort to retrieve Leif and reunite the family. They returned to the hospital the next day and her mother had passed in her absence.

The author was undone by grief and anguish after her mother's passing. Her relationship with her supportive husband, Paul, deteriorated and she was plagued by nightmares in which she killed her mother in graphic ways. The woman who loved her more than all the ten thousand things in the Tao Te Ching universe, plus ten thousand more, was gone forever and the author lost her place in the world.

Chapter 2: Splitting

A week after Strayed's mother died, her husband received an acceptance letter to attend a graduate program at the New School in New York City. She felt that she needed to stay in Minnesota to help keep her family together and that Paul should go on without her. However, he deferred for a year and by the time they went to New York it was clear that her family was drifting apart in the wake of the loss. The author was also having encounters with other men, and although they did not include sex, they did include romantic intimacy. In New York she wrote and worked as a waitress and continued to have affairs with men. However, Paul soon dropped out of graduate school and the couple moved to Portland after a cross country trip.

But the marriage continued to deteriorate. The author suggests this was because she was so personally lost. After Paul took a job in Minnesota, the author stayed in Portland and started having affairs with men that now included sex. Three years after her mother died she confessed the affairs to Paul and he moved out and the couple began a yearlong separation during which time they tried to decide if the marriage could be saved. The author felt torn in half as part of her wanted to save the marriage, and the other part was aware that she could not be what she needed to be to save it.

Chapter 3: Hunching in a Remotely Upright Position

The author was dropped off at a hotel in the Mojave dessert the night before she set out on the PCT. The next morning she dumped the contents of her pack on the bed and meticulously repacked it. She pondered the immensity of the task she was about to undertake, and grappled with the realization that she was profoundly inexperienced for the journey ahead. She had never, in point of fact, even been backpacking before.

The pack was unwieldy and heavy. Water sources were scarce on the first leg of the trail and so she packed a little over three gallons of water in two bottles and a dromedary bag. After struggling with her pack for a long time she finally got it so everything she had planned to take was in it or attached to the outside with bungee cords, but then found it was too heavy to lift. She had to sit on the floor and attach the bag and rock her body until momentum rested it on her back and then she struggled to stand. Finally on her feet, and unsteady, she walked out the door of the hotel room.

PART TWO: TRACKS

CHAPTER 4: THE PACIFIC CREST TRAIL, VOLUME 1: CALIFORNIA

The author needed a ride to the trail head so she left the hotel and made her way over to the gas station to hitch a ride. She finally worked up the nerve to ask two men for a ride and they dropped her at the trail head where she checked the trail register and added her name. Most of the other names were men in pairs. None of them were solo women. The weight of the pack was immediately an excruciating burden that she was clearly unprepared for. Uphill and downhill were both hard as balancing the pack, which was more than half her own weight, was a constant struggle. The sense that she was in over her head was a deafening roar by the time she had been on the trail for 45 minutes. She retold herself a different story – she was strong, brave and safe – until she believed it to be true. She pressed on.

In the year since her separation with Paul the author had an affair with a heroin addict named Joe and had been using the drug with him for a few months while in Portland. Her friend Lisa found out and told Paul who immediately drove from Minnesota to come confront her and get her away from the drugs. A month later, on a trip from Sioux Falls back to Minneapolis, the author realized she was pregnant and decided to have an abortion. She picked up a guide to the PCT trail a few months earlier but realized that she needed to leave as soon as she could. The book was called *The Pacific Crest Trail, Volume 1: California*. She had her abortion amidst a frantic push to prepare for the PCT.

Returning to her hike, the author shares that three hours into the walk she found a level spot with a boulder she could use to remove the pack. She was exhausted. The elevation was about 5,000 feet. She opened the guide book for reassurance. She sat in horror of how unready she was for this journey. She saw some sage, a plant she remembered from her childhood. She took some and rubbed the leaves between her hands, then inhaled deeply. It reminded her sharply of her mother. It strangely brought her comfort. She realized the worse thing in her life had already happened. She had lost her mother.

Chapter 5: Tracks

In the morning, after a fitful night's sleep in very windy conditions, the author awoke and forced herself to eat some granola with a powdered milk supplement. According to her guidebook the next water source was 13 miles ahead on the trail. After packing she set out only to find what appeared to be coyote or mountain lion scat within yards of her tent. She climbed over 1000 feet of trail by noon and the air had cooled by the time she had her protein bar and dried apricot lunch. Then she accidentally fell asleep and awoke a few hours later to rain drops and thick mist. She strapped on her pack and kept walking. Her shoulders and hips were being rubbed raw by the pack and her only thought was making forward progress.

By the evening she had reached a peak and the rain had turned to snow. By evening that day she had still not come upon the water source at Golden Oak Springs and she decided to pitch her tent and rest. She did, however, reach the spring within a few hours of setting off the next day. Covered with blisters and terribly sore, she stayed a full day at the spring. She used the day to learn how to use her compass and walk a short jeep trail to an overlook without her pack on. She also pulled out her stove to make a hot meal and discovered that she had purchased the wrong kind of fuel and it would not work.

On the fourth day Strayed fell while on the trail. Face down and under the full weight of the pack, she laid there for a moment to catch her breath. When she got up she saw that she had cut her leg and was bleeding heavily. After rinsing and stopping the bleeding with gauze, she resumed her hike. Eyes fixed on the trail now, she soon saw the tracks of a mountain lion traveling along the path not long ahead of her. On the fifth day she looked up and saw that she was being charged at by what at first she thought to be a moose, but later realized was a Texas longhorn bull. She dodged into some think brush and blew her whistle. The bull ran off.

She had run out of food that she could eat without cooking and decided to take a detour down some jeep roads to try to get to civilization and get the proper fuel for her stove. At the base of the mountain she came into a field where three men were sitting by a truck. They informed her that they were miners and that they were just getting ready to blow a hole in the mountain not far from where she just came.

Chapter 6: A Bull in Both Directions

One of the men took her home to his house where his wife made her some food. The next morning the man dropped her at a convenience store to catch a ride to a nearby town to get her stove fixed. She was standing at an intersection deciding on whether she should get a hotel for the night before returning to the trail, when she was approached by a homeless man on a child's bike. He offered her some of the bread and cold cuts that he had and wished her luck. She went to the grocery store to replace the food she had already eaten from her pack and found a motel.

The man that was running the desk at the hotel was a Vietnam veteran that noticed she was wearing a POW-MIA bracelet which her friend had given her before her journey. He gave her the only room with a tub and washed her clothes in the laundry for her. He also warned her that it was a record year for snowfall in the Sierra Nevada's. She was no stranger to snow having grown up in northern Minnesota. In addition, she had mailed an ice ax to the provisioning stop near Kennedy Meadows which was ahead of the severest part of the range. The next morning she returned to the PCT to resume her journey.

The terrain now was more open and she could see mountains in all directions, although she kept her eyes mainly on the trail for fear of another fall. At several points along the way, rockslides hindered her path. She was able to get past the treacherous obstacles at the cost of injuring her knee. She was now 7,000 feet in elevation. The views of the mountains were breathtaking and the air was warm even through the night. However, by the next day the heat was so unbearable because of the exposed trails that she thought she might not make it. She fantasized about quitting at the next reloading station, Kennedy Meadows, and pressed on.

She began to doubt the logic of the journey. While she had envisioned a kind of cathartic meditative time, it turned out that she was mostly occupied with the relentless pain of her body and matters of survival. Her mind would snag on bits of jingles that would get stuck in her head and run like a broken record. By the end of her first day back to the trail she made it to Spanish Needle Creek, and not having met anyone on the trail in her ten days on it, she felt empowered to strip naked and lay in the cool waters. The next morning she had another dip and decided she would give up and leave the trail at the next road crossing in 12 miles.

Just then a man approached and asked if she was Cheryl Strayed. Startled, she stammered out a yes. He explained he saw her name on the trail registry. His name was

Greg. He had prepared for this hike for years and was knowledgeable in all the ways she wasn't. He knew quite a bit about the trail and backpacking in general and Strayed intensely felt that her own ignorance was glaring. Then they talked about the snow on the high Sierras and Greg told her that many hikers had given up because of it. She thought this would make a great excuse for giving up but kept that to herself. Greg said he would be stopping over in Kennedy Meadows and they could meet up there to figure out a plan for the treacherous snowy mountains. When they parted on the trail he told her that he thought she was tough and that she would make it. This gave her just the motivation she needed to keep walking despite being humbled by the trail thus far. It was her new mantra for the next few days: *No one is tougher than me!*

A few days later, and nearly at Kennedy Meadows, Strayed saw her first bear twenty feet down the trail. Luckily when it saw her she blew her whistle and it turned and ran away. That same day she almost stepped on a rattlesnake. Despite her fears, the nearing of the end of the first leg of her journey made her realize that she was starting to bond with the trail. The next morning she awoke among the now familiar pains and stiffness that made it difficult to walk in the morning. Two men approached, a father and son named Albert and Matt. Again, they knew her name from the trail registry. They teased her good-naturedly about the size of her pack which was about the size of theirs combined, and soon left to return to the trail.

She realized that the challenges of this journey, perhaps the hardest thing she had ever done in many ways, made the difficulty of losing her mother and her marriage seem a little bit less hard. She shares how she changed her name to Cheryl Strayed when she and Paul finalized their divorce, and the final good byes of the pair on that fateful day, so full of mixed and deep emotions.

Chapter 7: The Only Girl in the Woods

At the store near Kennedy Meadows, the author picked up her provisions as well as a postcard from Joe stating that he wanted to get clean so that he could be her boyfriend someday. She was disappointed to have not heard from Paul, although still somewhat reminiscent for Joe. In addition she picked up a ski pole in a free box for PCT hikers. She hiked to the nearby campsite and found that she had just missed Greg, Albert and Matt who had caught a ride to the store. She was, however, preceded by her reputation as the man who was at the campground, Ed, knew her name and reputation as the woman with the gigantic pack.

Ed offered to share his food with her and after she washed up at the river she joined him at the picnic area. Ed was what was known as a trail angel, and each year he camped in Kennedy Meadows specifically to welcome the PCT hikers and assist as they passed through. The other men returned to the camp and, after a nap, Albert offered to help Strayed lighten her load. He sorted the contents of her pack into two piles, one to leave at the free box at the store or to mail home. Items in the discard pile included a foldable saw, the binoculars, a flash for the camera, books, and some toiletries.

After she repacked the items she would keep they shared stories about what brought them to the trail. Albert wanted to hike the trail as something that was important to him before dying, although still in his fifties. She told him that she thought it would be fun.

Doug and Tom, two hikers that were not far behind Strayed on the trail, caught up with the group at the campsite. Doug was handsome and friendly, and Strayed immediately felt some attraction to him. They were both what Strayed's mother would have referred to as New England blue bloods, from wealthy families in the northeast. She felt a kindred connection with the men, however, as it became clear they were, like her, novices at backpacking, and clearly shaken by the unexpected trials of the experience. When Tom took off his shoes at the campground, the author recognized the pain of his blistered feet with patches of skin coming off in in socks. She offered him some of the 2nd skin that she had in her pack and he gratefully accepted.

She spent some time in her tent pondering what it meant to be the only girl among six men in the woods. She was not practiced at being "just one of the guys" in social situations, although the context seemed to demand it of her. Being sweaty and dirty, without makeup or even deodorant, was no longer optional. She was interrupted by Doug who came to her tent and beckoned her to join him and the others at the river, and also gave her a gift of a long, black feather. At the water, the hikers discussed the snow and decided that they would go on for the next 40 miles of trail before making a decision on the worst part of the snow pack past Trail Pass.

The next day, Greg gave her a tutorial on how to use her ice ax. Doug and Tom watched on, while Albert and Matt seemed to be sick, possibly with giardia, which would require prescription medications to cure if true. They finally agreed to go to the doctor. On their way out of camp in Ed's truck, Strayed told Albert the real reasons she was hiking the trail: the death of her mother and her divorce from Paul had left her feeling lost in the world. She needed to find her bearings.

PART THREE: RANGE OF LIGHT

CHAPTER 8: CORVIDOLOGY

The next morning Strayed entered the gate to the High Sierra along with Doug and Tom. Ed was staying behind another day and would no doubt catch up with the author soon. Within a quarter of a mile from their start, Strayed made an excuse to stop and say goodbye to Doug and Tome because she wanted to hike alone. She had come to find a great deal of comfort being alone in the vastness. Her pack was lighter, although still a burden. Her body was still sore, but clearly also toughening to the conditions. The next 40 miles of trail included a nearly 5,000 feet rise in elevation.

By evening she had caught up with Doug and Tom and they pitched camp together. On the second day, again hiking alone, she came across a spot in the trail where snow and ice made a slick impasse across the trail. Falling would mean likely injury or even death. She made it across without incident but was reminded it was only a taste of what awaited ahead. It made her realize she would have to bypass the most treacherous parts of the PCT because she was simply not prepared for the record snows.

She shared her decision with Doug and Tom that night when they again met up for camp. They had decided to press on, and encouraged her to join them. She declined and later decided to add the 500 miles of trail in Oregon to her trek instead. The next day Greg caught up with her on the trail and told her that he too was bypassing the snowpack in the Sierra Nevada. In town she restocked and left a message with Lisa to hold her packages until she called with her new itinerary. She and Greg boarded a bus to Reno where they would catch another bus to Truckee, California, followed by catching rides for the final 45 miles to Sierra City. She had a little over 40 dollars to her name.

There was a small casino at the bus layover in Reno. Strayed was in the bathroom and a woman commented on her feather. She said it was likely from a corvid of some kind, a raven or a crow. These birds were symbols of the void, meaning the space where emptiness was churned into something new. They made it on to Sierra City and after paying for a hotel and dinner, Strayed was officially broke. She did, however, enjoy the luxury of a bath at the hotel and she had a $20 bill in her next care package that she would pick up at Belden Town soon. During her bath a blackened toenail came free of her foot, the first of several over the course of the next few weeks.

In bed that night she felt lonely. She pondered the memory of her biological father and his terrible fits of rage. She thought of her step father as well, a man that had more or less completely detached from her when her mother died. She thought about faith, and her lack of it.

Chapter 9: Staying Found

Strayed decided that her new goal was to make it to a place called the Bridge of the Gods which was over 1,000 trail miles away. She and Greg parted soon after arriving at the trail the next morning. Not long into her hike that day she came to a field of snow where the trail was no longer visible and Greg's footprints could not be found. She had left her ice ax back at the Sierra City post office thinking she would not need it for the next leg of the journey. She pressed on but soon started to panic that she had lost the trail all together. Finally she came across a trail marker letting her know that she was still on the trail, but there was still no sign of Greg.

The next day she hiked on, concerned all the while that she had lost the trail. When she stopped moving the temperature would make her shiver. She had to kick out footing in the snow and wished desperately for her ice ax. She also began feeling more and more lost and unsure of her bearings. Despite her fears, there was also an elation from the sense that she was truly alive. On her fourth day navigating the snow covered wilderness, she was sitting for a rest when a fox came to within ten feet of her and looked at her. She called quietly. "Fox." The fox looked at her for another moment and then trotted off. The she called loudly for her mother, surprising even herself.

The next day she came upon a jeep trail which let her know she was on the right track. However, the delay from the snow meant that she did not have enough supplies to make it to Belden Town. She would have to follow the jeep road down to the nearest town called Quincy. Along the way someone in an SUV headed for Packer Lack Lodge offered her a ride. The lodge was the opposite direction that she wanted to go but she accepted the ride.

Chapter 10: Range of Light

The lodge was a restaurant and the author left her pack outside while she went in, almost knocked over by the smells and longing for the food she had no money to buy. She talked with the manager inside about the snow on the trails who told her that many of the thru hikers were going around the trail in these parts and following the Gold Lake Highway to get around it. Disheartened, Strayed went back outside where she was approached by a woman, Christine, who had overheard her conversation about the PCT. She offered to let the author go back to the cabin and take a shower and have some food with her husband and teenaged children. She also traded her copy of Flannery O'Commor's *Complete Stories* for a copy of *The Novel* by James Michener who was one of her mother's favorites.

Then Christine drove her to the Quincy ranger station. The ranger was discouraging about the PCT because of the snow. However, the author found a ride across the street with some women going north to a place where the PCT crossed the road. On the drive she thought about Eddie, her stepfather, and the years before her mother died. There was a strong bond that was made even stronger during her mother's illness as the two joined forces in her care. But not long after her death he dethatched from her and her siblings and within a year had fallen in love with another woman and moved her and her children in to the house.

It was evening by the time she made it to the Whitehorse Campground some two miles from the PCT. Not long after setting up camp, she was informed by the managers of the campground that it was a 12 dollar fee to camp. They were not persuaded by her pleas that she had no money and they let her know that if she did not leave they would call the police. The batteries were dying in her flashlight by the time she was packed up and it was fully dark outside. She could barely follow the trail in the dark but was able to make it to a clearing about 20 minutes later where she set up camp. She laid in the dark and remembered when herself, Paul and Leif had the duty of killing her mother's sick horse who was dying not long after her mother's death. Leif fired the shots but the horse still struggled in agony for several minutes before finally dying.

The next morning she realized there was an alternate route through lower elevation less likely to be snow bound. At camp that night she ran into three men that offered her what they called Hawaiian screwdrivers, fresh trout, chips and guacamole. They marveled at the story of her solo journey on the PCT. The next day she hobbled into the Belden Town post office to pick up her package and bought to Snapple teas. A woman by the name of Trina approached her on the porch and asked her if she was hiking the PCT. She reported that she had turned back from the trail north of the PCT because of the snow, which dampened Strayed's spirits. Another woman, Stacy, was also hiking the trail. The three decided to camp together and forge a plan. They ran into another PCT hiker named Brent, who she had heard about from the folks at Kennedy Meadows. She enquired about Greg and he told her that he had abandoned the PCT because of the snow. The four of them had dinner and discussed the fact that huge swaths of the trail ahead were socked in with snow. They decided on a trek that would bypass the worst of the snow.

PART FOUR: WILD

CHAPTER 11: THE LOU OUT OF LOU

The author hiked 50 miles with Stacy and Trina to a town called Chester where they hitched a ride north. There was not enough room in the ride for all of them so Strayed stayed behind to catch her own ride. While waiting for a ride, a reporter doing a piece on those living the hobo life asked if he could interview her. She tried to explain that she was not a hobo, but instead a long distance hiker, but the difference seemed to be lost on him. After the interview and a picture, the man handed her what he called a care package containing a beer and some food items she immediately consumed after he drove off. Soon after she hitched a ride to Old Station where she planned to meet up with the other hikers.

The three women reunited and planned their next leg together through a 30 mile dry stretch of trail known as Hat Creek Rim. The next morning the other women left camp early and Strayed lagged behind wanting to hike alone. She ended up staying another day, spending time in the campground doing some writing, and then going into town to spend the last of her money on dinner. At the last minute, she decided to call

Paul from a payphone. They talked for nearly an hour in an easy friendly way. She appreciated that they were still close, but she also felt some peace that all the things that got her to where she was now, were things she needed to do, including divorcing Paul. She felt like only now was she really getting into what this trip was about for her.

Chapter 12: This Far

The next morning at first light the author packed her bag, which she could now do in five minutes, and hit the trail. She had bonded with the pack, naming it Monster, and feeling now as if the two of them were in this together. Carrying the weight of the pack had changed her body and made her strong. She felt sure she was finally past all of the snow and her trek forward would be more seamless. The weather was hot and this stretch had only one water source for 30 miles. When she saw the water tank come into view she finished the last few swallows of water she had in her canteen. When she got up to it, she realized the tank was empty. She was terrified. The temperature was above 100 degrees. She consorted her guide book. The book said there was a questionable reservoir another 5 miles up the trail. The author had no choice but to seek it out.

About the time the sun was setting she came upon the reservoir. The water was murky and full of sludge. She used her water purifier pump and added iodine to the water for extra insurance. After drinking four bottles of the water, and too exhausted to pitch a tent, she laid down on a tarp and fell asleep under the moon. She awoke two hours later covered in tiny black frogs jumping along her body. She hustled out of their path and set up her tent yards away.

The next day she broke off the trail to a small town called Cassel because she knew she would not make it to the next water source that day. She had 76 cents, not enough to buy a Snapple tea. The cashier let her have a Snapple anyway and let her set up camp behind the store. A little later a PCT hiker named Rex was dropped off at the store with his pack. He looked at her boots and suggested she call the store where she got them because they offered a full guarantee. The next day she arrived at the McArthur-Burney Falls Memorial State Park where she picked up her provisions and called REI, the retailer for the shoes, who agreed to mail her a new pair free of charge. She also ran into Trina at the store and they all followed her back to the campsite where Stacy was waiting.

Her feet were in terrible shape. Her big toes were so swollen that she could see the blood circulating in them. She hoped that the new boots, one size larger, would help. She found that by removing the nails she experienced immediate relief from the worst of the throbbing pain. The next day she went back to the store to wait for her boots to arrive. There were tourists that came and went and sometimes they gathered around and asked her questions about the PCT. She felt a good deal of pride and confidence relating her tales. When the boots did not arrive she called REI and discovered they had not mailed them yet because they were not able to overnight them there and so they would have to mail them to her next provisioning site, 83 trail miles away.

Chapter 13: The Accumulation of Trees

Strayed decided to try walking in her sandals instead of her boots. The soles were flimsy and she could feel each pebble beneath her feet, but the boots were much more painful to wear because of her toes smashing up against them. The trail near Castle Crags was rough, however, and by the next day she had to don the boots despite the excruciating pain. She stopped on the trail near a ledge for a rest and to massage her feet. Just in that moment her pack fell over and knocked one of the boots over the ledge, lost now forever. In frustration she hurled the other boot over the ledge. She had no choice but to tape together the sandals which were falling apart, and move on.

The next day she came into some clear-cut land where the trees were being cut for wood. The downed trees, upturned earth, and multiple crisscrossing roads made the trail at first difficult, then impossible, to follow. By lunchtime she was officially lost. Her sandals were falling apart so she made duct tape booties by rolling the tape around her socks and then securing them to the sandals. The next day she decided to just follow one of the logging roads to wherever it took her believing that eventually it would lead to civilization. It eventually lead to a highway where she hitched a ride back to the PCT a few miles north after answering some questions about her duct tape booties.

The next day she arrived at the Castle Crags provisioning spot, almost barefoot from her disintegrating booties. In addition to her new boots there were nine letters awaiting her. Joe, Paul and her sister Karen had all written, along with several other friends across the country. She also ran into Rex and Stacy along with others she had met on the trail, several of whom had also gotten lost among the clear cut section of the trail and had hitched a ride to this provisioning spot. They spent the evening socializing and Strayed got drunk by accident. The next morning Rex reminded her there were only about 200 miles to go before Oregon, which she considered with mixed feelings.

Chapter 14: Wild

It turned out that the new boots were a blessing and a curse. While they did relieve her from the searing pain in her toes, new spots rubbed raw. She pushed through the day in agony, stopping briefly to nap and dream that Bigfoot had kidnapped her. Later that evening she caught up with the others. They discussed that there was a Rainbow Gathering up ahead at Toad Lake. She decided she would go there and let her feet rest for a few days. Besides, there would be free food there. However, the next day when they arrived at the site where it should have been, they did not find the gathering.

Back on the trail a few days later, Strayed stopped by a spring in a meadow. She was soaking her feet when a white llama with a pack and a halter came bounding up to her. She grabbed the halter trying to sooth the animal and moments later a gray haired woman named Vera and small child named Kyle came up to introduce themselves and thank her for catching the llama. They chatted for a short while and Strayed returned to the trail. She decided not to meet up with the group for the next several nights, ready now again to be alone through the night. One such night she stopped and enjoyed a sunset. She felt full and complete. She cried her first tears on the trail that night.

PART FIVE: BOX OF RAIN

CHAPTER 15: BOX OF RAIN

After two months in California, the author finally made it to the border of Oregon in chilly and rainy weather. There was a registry box at the border and she looked through the entries and saw the familiar names of some of the people she had met in her travels. Stacy had turned back after her gear was soaked through, but the author had made plans to meet her at a hostel in Ashland. Ashland was originally planned as the last stop on her journey. The resupply box waiting for her there contained 250 dollars and clean clothes, along with another resupply box that she had Lisa send from one of the missed stops in the Sierra Nevada. When she arrived at Ashland she found out that Jerry Garcia, of the famed band The Grateful Dead, had died. Youth were congregated in small groups along the streets and she learned that some sort of memorial celebration had been planned. When she arrived at the post office, the woman at the counter handed her only an envelope and told her that there was no box there for her. She had less than three dollars. The envelope had a necklace made by a friend of hers with her name "Strayed" engraved on it, although ironically the "Y" looked more like a "V" to most that noticed it. She called Lisa to find out about the box but there was no answer.

She returned to the post office a few hours later and the same woman behind the counter went in the back again and produced her box. She went with Stacy back to the hostel and showered and dressed in her clean clothes. They headed for the Jerry Garcia memorial after having dinner. She met a man named Jonathan at the event and made a date for the next day at a Wilco show that he was working at.

After the Wilco show the next day, she met Jonathan for their date. He took her out to the organic farm where he lived. She found she was very attracted to him. He lived in a large tent constructed on a platform on the farm where he worked for free lodging. They had no condoms so they decided not to have sex, but they enjoyed each other's bodies in the many other ways available to them. The next day they took a long trip to a beach that was a long drive away. The author felt somewhat out of sorts being so far from the PCT. She realized when they finally arrived at the beach that she had been there years before with Paul. She walked off alone for a while, bending to write Paul's name in the sand, something she had done every time the two of them were at the beach. She stopped to consider the value of forgiving herself for all of the things she had done to wrong him. What if she just allowed for all those wrongs to be what she needed to do in those times to make her who she was today?

She rejoined Jonathan on the Beach. They had lunch and afterwards, now with condoms at hand, they found a secluded spot protected from view by some boulders, and made love. He took her back to the hostel after the long drive back. They said goodbye and although she was grateful for the lovely time with him, the author felt somewhat empty. The next day she packed up and headed once again for the PCT.

Chapter 16: Mazama

The author now had in her possession *The Pacific Crest Trail, Volume 2: Oregon and Washington.* The terrain during the first few days beyond Ashland was deeply forested and did not have the panoramic views the author had become accustomed to on most of the PCT trail to this point. The weather turned cool with the elevation now near 6,000 feet. She had to keep moving to stay warm. She spent August 18th alone in the cold mountains. It was her mother's birthday and she pondered how she would have been 50 years old had she lived. She was feeling anger at her mother for not having lived. As she walked on the rage got stronger. She made a list in her head of all of the other failings that she could think of that her mother had over the years. Then she stopped walking and wailed into the empty expanse. How could she forgiver her for all her failings and when she had left her so prematurely? It would always be unfinished, always an emptiness that the author could never fill.

She sat on a rock and noticed some crocus, a flower that grew at the spot where she had spread the ashes of her mother. The anger started to abate, and she began to see that of course her mother was an amazing mother. She started to feel the gratitude of having had such a wonderful mother. By that evening she had arrived at a new peace.

A few days later she arrived at Crater Lake National Park, which was crawling with tourists. The next day she hiked to the lake and stood at a point some 900 feet above the surface of the water. The lake reflected back the purest blue she had ever seen. She stood transfixed and felt the power of the place. She had to stay until the next day when the office would be open so she could pick up her box. She thought about her mother and her words in the final days of her life lamenting on the fact that always a daughter, a wife, a mother. She had never been in charge of her own life. She thought about the lake, once a 12,000 foot tall volcano that when it erupted to form the lake had lost its heart. She felt strangely at peace in this land.

Chapter 17: Into a Primal Gear

She had two provisioning stops left before her final destination now a mere 334 trail miles from the Bridge of the Gods. A special treat of the last leg was that there were several varieties of edible berries now ripening all along the trail. Her feet still hurt terribly, but the weight of her pack was getting easier to bear. She likened the final few legs of the trail to a game of hopscotch. Somewhat bored of the monotony of the trail she walked in a primal gear with only the thought of arriving at her next destination and checking off one more leg of the journey.

At Shelter Cove Resort she stopped to camp and shower while waiting for the post office to open the next morning. While sitting on the porch of the little store at the park three male PCT hikers approached her and asked if she was Cheryl. They had been following her on the trail for some time, thinking that they might catch up with her soon. Rick, Richie and Josh were their names. They had started in Mexico and hiked all the way through the Sierra Nevada, despite the record snow. Their trail-name was the "Three Young Bucks." When she got her box the next day, it was missing the 20 dollars she was counting on. With under seven dollars she hiked out with the Three Young Bucks. Soon they broke off and she was alone again. After a brief detour to Elk Lake resort, where she spent all but her last two pennies on a cheeseburger and fries, she continued on. She felt some gratitude for the way that growing up so poor had given her the confidence to keep moving forward without money in a way that most people would have surely balked at.

She continued hiking through the Three Sisters, stopping to talk to the more frequent day hikers along that stretch of the trail. Most of the people asked her all kinds of questions about her trip. A few days later she was alone again as she entered the Mount Jefferson Wilderness. In a few days she would reach Olallie Lake, the last provisioning stop on her journey.

One afternoon she ran across some bow hunters who had underestimated how much fluid to bring on their day trip and were rather desperate for water. She let them use her water purifier to get some water out of the nearby pond. Unfortunately, the hunter allowed the intake tube to suck up the muck at the bottom of the water and it had completely jammed the filter. The man was notably unapologetic about ruining her water filter. She then gave them some iodine pills to put water in the empty soda cans to drink. The men were rude and sexist and she started to feel unsafe as they talked about her figure and how it was dangerous for a woman to be out here alone as if she was not even present. She was relieved when they started back to their truck. She suggested that she would be right behind them but once they were out of site she started pitching her tent planning to stay near the pond for the night.

She was shocked when one of the men reappeared a short time later after having likely watched her change her clothes. He made suggestive comments about how nice she looked and she tried to make clear that she was very uncomfortable with his presence while she ran through in her head any defensive weapons she could get her hands on in the event he attacked her, settling on grabbing one of the arrows from the pack on his back and stabbing him in the throat if need be. After a few minutes she heard his friend calling for him and then appearing through the bushes beckoning his friend to come on back to the truck, obviously annoyed. After the men left, Strayed was unable to calm down. She packed and started hiking out even though the dark was close upon her. It got darker still, and then she started running.

Chapter 18: Queen of the PCT

It was raining the next day when she woke up in the light after pitching her tent late the night before. It rained off and on through the next day when she finally reached Olallie Lake. She arrived after the store closed and set up camp nearby as she fantasized about the contents in her last provision box. She also thought about Portland where she had finally decided she would live after the PCT was behind her. The next day she got her box and three letters. One was from Paul, another from a friend Aimee, and much to her surprise, the third was from Ed, the trail angel that she met at Kennedy Meadows. Her box also contained two twenty dollar bills, which solved the mystery of the missing bill from the last box.

She decided to stay the night and join some of the staff for dinner that evening. In the meantime she did her best to dry her clothes and repair her water pump. Right before dinner the Three Young Bucks strode into camp. She had already accepted a dinner invitation from the staff who would not have enough food for the men, so she went and had some casserole and smuggled out a piece of cake for the guys. The ranger had invited her to his home for a drink after dinner, and she consented only if he would allow the Bucks to also come. She managed to keep a safe distance from the ranger who was clearly drunk and interested in her, long enough for the four PCT hikers to enjoy the warm fire and some libations, before heading back to camp.

The next morning the Three Young Bucks informed her that they had a trail name for her: "The Queen of the PCT." Around that time, the man at the store offered to let the hikers have a cabin for a cheap deal and they accepted. After setting up the cabin, they returned to the store. Strayed's friend Lisa from Portland was standing there by the woodstove. The women jumped with delight when they saw each other. The author felt mixed feelings because it was good to see her friend, but it also signaled the near end of her PCT adventure. Then the Young Bucks, Lisa, Lisa's boyfriend Jason, and the author piled into Lisa's truck and headed to the nearby Bagby Hot Springs for a soak in the warm mineral waters there.

Chapter 19: The Dream of a Common Language

The next morning the Bucks left before she awoke. The ranger caught her and delivered a package from her friend Gretchen which contained a bottle of red wine and a box of fine chocolates. Just then she heard someone calling her name and she turned to find Doug running to catch up with her. He and Tom had done some of the snowy Sierra Nevada and then decided to detour about halfway through. That night they made camp together near Warm Springs River and Strayed shared her chocolates and wine. It felt like a ceremonial end to such a long journey. After Doug turned in for the night, the author thought of her step father Eddie and focused on what he had given her instead of the sad fact of his detachment after her mother's death. He had been the one to take her camping and taught her how to pitch a tent.

A few days later they were joined by Tom who had caught up from behind. They were also joined by two women and their party went together to the Timberline Lodge of Mount Hood. She was fifty trail miles from the Bridge of the Gods and she wanted to set off on her own for the last leg of the journey. She said goodbye to Doug and Tom, later the two women, and was once again alone in the forest. She spent the last night of the trek on the banks of the Eagle Creek, six short miles from the Bridge of the Gods. Relaxing by the river that evening, she pulled off the sixth loose toenail.

The next day she arrived at the Columbia River and soon after the Bridge of the Gods. She stood on the near side of the bridge and did not cross the river. She stayed there for a while, and then went to a nearby ice-cream shop and spent her last two dollars on a cone. She sat at the store and took her time knowing her next task would be to hitch a ride to Portland and begin her new life.

Four years later she would return to this spot and cross the river on the Bridge of the Gods to marry a man. They would come to have a son Carter, and a daughter Bobbi, named after her mother. Fifteen years later they would all return to this spot and have ice cream, and only then would the full meaning of her hike be revealed to her, although even then it was deeper than words would allow for.

ANALYSIS

Wild offers the reader both outdoor adventure and reflexive introspection in great depth and balance. Cheryl Strayed has offered up a gripping and honest tale that bares the realities of both her physical and emotional struggles along the 1,100 miles she hiked of the Pacific Crest Trail. The story is vivid in imagery and an inspiring tale of person triumph.

A strength of the prose is that it is immediately accessible and friendly. There is no air of pretention as the author makes clear her own ignorance right from the start. This gives the story an inviting appeal for those readers that don't have the language of experienced backpackers. The down side of this, however, is that readers seeking a more technical perspective of surviving on the trail will be disappointed.

Like the rough and winding terrain of the PCT, the author does meander a bit. There are times when the intertwining of the literal and the metaphorical feel forced and contrived, but other times when they come together with a striking, natural synergy. Like weeks of one foot in front of the other, the story sometimes gets repetitive, only to turn a corner to reveal a jewel of a revelation.

The author is strikingly most passionate in describing her mother, and the visceral devastation that Strayed felt when she died. She clearly demonstrates the healing that occurred as she faced her own trials on the trail and made forward progress despite the many hardships she faced. The sense that the physical strain of the ordeal forced the author to be so present and grounded in the moment that she found herself through this act of endurance is palpable. However, tangential stories of grief such as her father, step-father and ex-husband are not woven as tightly into the main narrative and leave the reader sensing loose ends.

One disappointment of the book is the sense that we are headed for a major cathartic destination, only to find a very brief summary chapter lacking in revelations. Perhaps this was the author's intent, but that does not soften the anticlimactic ending of the book. What is worse is that there is an allusion that she has discovered a great meaning from the journey now, decades later, but she then fails to share that clearly with the reader.

Most readers, however, will find the value of the book to be the vivid descriptions of the scenery and people she encounters on her journey. We are reminded of the value of simple acts of kindness in the lives of those struggling around us and the beauty in the world that is there for the viewing. Most will find her bravery and endurance to be inspiring. The biggest take away from the story is that we have to keep moving in our lives, even when the terrain is rough, the pain seems unbearable, and the road ahead is unclear.

Made in the USA
San Bernardino, CA
27 July 2019